THE SECRET TASTE OF LOVE

DAVID and ANNIE TOBOROWSKY

David and Annie Toborowsky are the beloved couple known for their heartfelt journey on TLC's 90-Day Fiancé, where their love story flourished despite cultural challenges and personal trials. David, from Louisville, Kentucky, met Annie during a transformative trip to Thailand while grappling with financial struggles, a painful divorce, and health issues, including a stroke. Annie, a vibrant woman from a small town in Thailand, brought renewed hope and purpose to David's life.

After their engagement, they faced the daunting task of securing Annie's K-1 visa to bring her to the U.S. Upon moving, Annie clung to her cooking to bridge the gap between her Thai heritage and her new life in America. Food had always represented love and tradition for her. In her kitchen, she recreated cherished dishes that connected her to home.

As David faced unemployment and financial pressures, Annie's cooking became their sanctuary. One memorable evening, when David was feeling particularly low, Annie surprised him with a feast of his favorite Thai dishes: Spicy Tom Yum Soup, jasmine rice, Pad Thai, and her famous Thai Basil Stir fry. The meal, filled with the rich aromas of their culture, was a heartfelt reminder of their bond and the love they shared.

Their relationship faced some skepticism, but Annie's unwavering belief in David, along with her ability to find joy in simple moments helped them overcome obstacles. David took on various jobs to help rebuild his life, determined to create a stable home for Annie.

Today, they thrive personally and professionally, captivating audiences as fan favorites on TLC's 90-Day Fiancé. Annie's passion for cooking has led her to share recipes and cooking segments, blending their cultures and spreading joy. Their story is a testament to resilience, illustrating that love, hard work, and faith can triumph over challenges. Together, they show that home is wherever they are, rooted in love, laughter, and the flavors of life.

ISBN: 978-1-998532-28-5

For permission requests, write to the publisher:

Ahelia Publishing, LLC
Box 532 Augusta, MT 59410

support@aheliapublishing.org
www.aheliapublishing.org

Published in the United States of America
Printed in the United States of America

David & Annie

A FEW OF OUR FAVORITE
Recipes

Chicken Dishes

Country Thai BBQ Chicken   10

Gang Pa Jungle Curry   14

Khao Soi   18

Penang Curry with Chicken   22

Thai Basil Chicken Stir Fry   28

Green Curry with Chicken   32

Chicken with Lemongrass   36

Laab Chicken   42

Chicken Soup with
Tomato & Potato   46

Matzah Ball Chicken Soup   50

Vegetable Dishes

Papaya Salad   58

Som Tom Thai   62

Fried Spring Rolls   66

Stuffed Mushrooms   72

Kai jiao   76

Cauliflower with Egg   80

Pork Dishes

Khao Tom (Rice Soup)   86

Issan Sausages   90

Pumpkin Red Curry   94

Seafood Dishes

Tom Yum Goong   100

Stir Fried Yellow Curry Seafood   104

DISHES WITH
Chicken

Country Thai bbq Chicken

In the heart of rural Thailand, where emerald fields stretch out like a patchwork quilt and the air buzzes with the song of cicadas, a special day arrives only a few times each year. It is not specifically marked on any calendar, but more by the enticing aromas that waft through the air—a scent of magic and celebration. This was the day our village came alive with the sizzling fragrance of *Thai Country BBQ Chicken*.

I remember those days vividly, each memory etched in my heart like the sun warming the earth. The adults would bustle about, preparing a variety of traditional dishes. They mixed spicy chicken salad, known as laab, and brewed rich chicken soup infused with herbs that made your taste buds dance. But for me, as a young child, my mouth watered for one thing: *Thai BBQ Chicken*.

While the grown-ups approached their cooking with solemn reverence, I was consumed with pure joy at the sight of the chicken roasting over an open flame. The crackling sound was music to my ears, filling me with anticipation.

As the skin crisped to a golden perfection, the secret marinade—a perfect blend of sweet and savory—created a symphony of flavors that still lingers in my daydreams.

On those very special days, the meal transcended mere sustenance; it was a celebration wrapped in warmth and shared stories. The village gathered, and when the BBQ chicken made its grand entrance, everyone's eyes sparkled with delight. We dug in with gusto, savoring each bite like the most precious gift that it truly was.

I can still picture the scene: families huddled together, children darting between tables, and laughter ringing like a joyous chorus. The sun bathed us in golden light, and the air was thick with the love and connection that only such gatherings can bring.

Each morsel of chicken was savored, every shared smile deepening the bonds that tied us together from those days of the past to these days of the present.

As the days would fade into evening, laughter echoed into the twilight, and the stars emerged like tiny gems in the night sky. Those meals were more than just food; they were moments of togetherness, joy wrapped in the irresistible allure of *Thai Country BBQ Chicken.*

Whenever that familiar scent wafts through the air, I am transported right back to those cherished moments—the laughter, the love, and the simple pleasure of being together. It serves as a reminder that amidst the hustle of life, the shared meals and connections we nurture genuinely feed our souls and bind us together.

Each time I catch that aroma, I'm reminded of my roots, the village that shaped me, and the love that continues to flavor my life. For these reasons, I share my recipe of *Country Thai BBQ Chicken* with you.

Country Thai bbq Chicken

SPICES & SAUCES:

1 tablespoon salt

1 tablespoon soy sauce

1 tablespoon oyster sauce

1/2 tablespoon sugar

INGREDIENTS:

3 chicken thighs

5 cloves of peeled garlic

2 pieces of lemongrass - sliced

DIRECTIONS:

- Wash chicken thighs.
- Slice lemongrass on an angle.
- Moto the peeled garlic together with lemongrass.
- Slice openings in the chicken to absorb the ingredients.
- Add lemongrass and garlic paste to the chicken.
- Mix together the salt, oyster sauce, soy sauce, and sugar.
- Spoon over chicken, ensuring plenty of mixture seeps into the open slices.
- Add any other ingredients you desire, to achieve your preferred taste.
- Refrigerate for 1-3 hours.
- Cook on BBQ grill until thoroughly cooked.

Gang Pa Jungle Curry

You know those moments when you sit down with someone you care about and have one of those, "Let's be healthy" talks? That was me with David, my beloved partner, as we sat in our cozy kitchen. The late afternoon sun streamed in through the window, casting a warm glow over our cluttered countertops. I looked at him, his face a mix of determination and dread, and I knew it was time for a change.

"David," I said, my voice light but firm, "it's time to get serious about your health. You've been living off pizza and hotdogs! We need to make some changes."

He chuckled, rubbing his stomach playfully. "But I'm too busy! I don't have time to cook healthy meals."

I flashed him my sweetest, most mischievous smile. "I want to make you soup! But not just any soup... this one will help you get fit!"

His eyes lit up at the word *Soup*. "Alright, Annie, let's do this. I love soup. How bad can it be?"

I grinned wider, feeling the excitement bubbling within me. "Oh, trust me, David. It's going to be spicy."

"Spicy?" His confidence wavered slightly, but he tried to play it cool. "No problem, I like a little heat."

With that, I jumped into action, diving into our pantry like a treasure hunter. I pulled out magical ingredients: Thai eggplant, kaffir lime leaves, fiery Thai bird chilis, and a jar of Jungle Curry Paste that I claimed was special from my hometown. The colors and scents filled the kitchen.

David's eyes widened as I added two hefty spoonfuls of the curry paste into the pot. "How spicy is this really?" he asked, a bead of sweat forming on his forehead.

"Very spicy!" I beamed, stirring as the rich red liquid bubbled and simmered, sending tantalizing scents wafting through the room. "Perfect for your diet!"

Once the soup was ready, I ladled a small portion into a bowl and presented it to David like a prized, 5-star dish. He hesitated and took a spoonful. Almost instantaneously, his face turned redder than a lobster. Sweat beaded on his brow, and his eyes widened in shock. "Annie... this is lava!" he exclaimed, fanning his face dramatically.

I couldn't help but laugh, the sound bubbling up like the soup itself. "You said you wanted to lose weight! Spicy food boosts metabolism!"

He took another courageous bite, his mouth already on fire. "I think I'm losing consciousness, not weight!" he joked, but I could see determination in his eyes.

To my surprise, he kept eating. With each bowl, I encouraged him with my big smile and promises of a *flat stomach*. "Just think of it as a cleanse!" I said, my heart swelling with pride at his perseverance.

In the end, David devoured three bowls of that spicy *Jungle Curry Soup*. He didn't lose weight that day but lost his taste for spicy food forever. As we sat together, laughter ringing through our kitchen, I realized that even amidst the heat, there was warmth in sharing a meal—an experience that brought us closer, one spicy bite at a time.

Gang Pa Jungle Curry

SPICES AND SAUCES:

fresh black peppercorn with stem

1/2 bunch Thai basil or hot basil

Thai bird chilis - 2 or 3 pieces

1-2 tablespoons red curry paste

2 cups water

2 tablespoons fish sauce

INGREDIENTS:

1/2 pound chicken thighs

5 Thai eggplants, cut into 1/4 inch pieces

1 bunch long green beans, cut into 1/4 inch pieces

5-8 baby corn, cut into small pieces

2 carrots, sliced into small pieces

1/2 zucchini, cut into small pieces

pumpkin or squash, cut into small pieces

5 pieces kaffir lime leaf

DIRECTIONS:

- Add water to a pot and turn temperature to high heat.
- Add Thai eggplant, beans, pumpkin, zucchini, carrots, and baby corn.
- Add red curry paste.
- Lower temperature to just over medium heat.
- Cook for 5-7 minutes.
- Add chicken.
- Cook for another 5 minutes or until chicken is cooked.
- Add fish sauce, chicken stock, sugar, and Thai bird chilis.
- Turn off temperature.
- Add basil, kaffir lime leaf, and pepper corn.
- Serve with jasmine rice - or brown rice for a healthier option.
- Adjust taste to your spice level.

Khao Soi

Growing up in the vibrant Isaan region of Thailand, my childhood was steeped in local flavors. Our family table showcased dishes like *Som Tam*, the zesty papaya salad bursting with lime and fresh vegetables, and larb, the spicy minced meat salad that brought warmth to our meals. Yet, one dish remained a tantalizing mystery—*Khao Soi*.

This coconut curry noodle soup, often highlighted in movies and travel shows, was a distant dream, a flavor I had yet to experience. I would watch TV characters savor its creamy goodness, imagining the symphony of tastes within its golden depths.

My culinary journey began when I met my husband, David. With his adventurous spirit and love for food, he guided me into a world of flavors beyond my upbringing. Our trip to Chiang Mai ignited a spark; I could finally try *Khao Soi,* the dish that had captured my imagination. The anticipation was palpable.

As we wandered the colorful streets of Chiang Mai, the air was thick with the enticing aroma of spices and simmering curries. Suddenly, the scent of *Khao Soi* beckoned us to a bustling local eatery. My heart raced as I stepped inside, enveloped by the vibrant atmosphere.

When the dish arrived, it was a sight to behold. The golden curry glistened under the soft light, tender chicken nestled in creamy coconut milk, and crispy noodles crowned it like a queen. It was a moment of pure joy and discovery.

As I lifted my spoon, the first bite was a revelation. The harmonious blend of spices—lemongrass, turmeric, and coriander—enveloped my tongue. The richness of the coconut milk wrapped around me like a comforting blanket. The sweet crunch of the crispy noodles created a delightful contrast, making each flavor dance on my palate. I closed my eyes, savoring the moment, feeling like I had uncovered a long-searched-for, hidden treasure.

Sharing this experience with David made it even more profound. We exchanged smiles and laughter, every bite deepening our connection, weaving our stories together through food. With every spoonful, we created memories that would linger long after the last drop was savored.

In that bowl of *Khao Soi*, I found more than just a delicious dish; I discovered a bridge between my childhood memories and future adventures. It was a connection to the broader culinary landscape of Thailand, a testament to the love we shared through food.

As the sun dipped below the horizon, casting a warm glow over Chiang Mai, I realized that *Khao Soi* was not merely a meal. It represented exploration, the joy of sharing, and the profound connections forged through eating. Every flavor and shared bite had the power to transform a simple experience into something extraordinary—an unforgettable moment I would carry with me forever.

Khao Soi

SPICES and SAUCES:

3 tablespoons red curry paste

2 tablespoons Massaman curry paste

1 tablespoon salt

2 tablespoons fish sauce

2 tablespoons palm or brown sugar

INGREDIENTS:

1 pound chicken leg or beef shoulder - cubed

500 ml coconut milk

1 package egg noodles - fresh or dry

1 cup vegetable oil (for deep frying)

Condiments to Serve with Dish:

pickled cabbage

chopped red onion

cilantro

limes

crunchy egg noodle

dry chili flakes

DIRECTIONS:

Massaman Curry Soup:

- In large pot, add 750 ml water with 250 ml coconut milk, bring to boil.
- Add 1 tablespoon salt and the chicken or beef; lower heat to medium.
- In a Wok or fry pan, heat 250 ml coconut milk to bubbling; lower temperature.
- To Wok or frypan, add the Massaman and red curry.
- Mix together thoroughly for 3-4 minutes.
- Add mixture to the pot—cook on medium until meat is thoroughly cooked.
- Taste before adding sugar and fish sauce, then add according to your desired taste.

Cook Egg Noodles:

- Deep fry 1 bunch of egg noodles in oil for 10 seconds to make the noodle crunchy.
- Remove and let cool, drying with paper towel to remove excess oil.
- Boil the egg noodles in boiling water 1-3 minutes, or to desired finish.
- In bowl, add cooked egg noodles, soup ingredients with meat, topped by condiments.

Penang Curry with Chicken

I had always been a dreamer, my heart was alive with the colors and possibilities of the world. Yet, growing up in a small village in Thailand, reality often felt like a heavy weight pressing down on my aspirations. After finishing school, I worked in a bustling factory in Bangkok, earning a meager $200 monthly. It wasn't very much, but it was my only opportunity at the time. Each long day in the factory left me exhausted, my hands sore from the repetitive motions, the relentless rhythm of machinery echoing in my ears.

Despite the weariness settling in my bones, I clung to the small joys that kept my spirit alive. One of those joys was food—a connection to my roots, a burst of flavor that could transport me beyond the factory walls. In my village, meals were simple: rice, stir frys, and soups that nourished the body but rarely excited the palate. Yet, I knew a world of flavors awaited me, a world I had yet to explore.

One fateful day, a colleague invited me to lunch at a nearby restaurant as the sun shone through the factory windows. My heart raced with anticipation; it was a chance to step outside of my routine. When the dish arrived, it felt like a gift from the universe. *Penang Curry*, a rich, creamy coconut-based dish vibrant in color and fragrant, embraced me with its warm aroma.

As I took that first bite, my eyes widened in wonder. The explosion of flavors was unlike anything I had ever tasted. The tender chicken melted in my mouth, the spices danced on my tongue, and the smooth texture of the coconut milk enveloped my senses.

With each bite, I felt I had discovered a new world filled with richness and depth that I had long been denied. In my village, dishes like *Penang Curry* were rare treats, luxuries reserved for special occasions, not something families could afford regularly.

Savoring each mouthful, I felt the contrast between the curry's heat and its cooling creaminess. This beautiful harmony mirrored my journey. At that moment, sitting in a bustling restaurant, I realized just how much I had grown. I had come from a small village where opportunities felt very limited. Nevertheless, here I was in Bangkok, tasting something exquisite that felt like a celebration of life itself. This culinary journey was about discovering a new dish and uncovering a part of myself I never knew existed.

A soft smile crept onto my lips as gratitude filled my heart. I promised myself then and there that I would someday share this dish with others—perhaps with my family back home, introducing them to the flavors that had opened my eyes to the wonders of the world beyond our tiny village. It was a moment I would never forget, a simple lunch that made me feel like I had unearthed something extraordinary, a glimpse of the dreams I dared to hold onto. This dish, I knew, was not just a meal, but a story waiting to be told.

Penang Curry with Chicken

SPICES and SAUCES:

2.5 tablespoons Penang curry

2 tablespoons brown or palm sugar

3 tablespoons fish sauce

3 red chilis, sliced

INGREDIENTS:

1 pound chicken breast sliced into small pieces

1 can coconut milk

8 kaffir lime leaves

DIRECTIONS:

- Add ½ can of coconut milk to a pot, turn heat to medium.
- Let boil and stir the coconut milk until it reduces to the oil.
- Add Penang curry to the pot and mix thoroughly.
- Add ¼ cup of coconut milk and stir with red curry.
- Add chicken to the pot.
- Turn heat up to medium to allow chicken to cook.
- Add 1 cup of water.
- Continue mixing and let chicken cook thoroughly.
- After chicken is cooked, add sugar and fish sauce.

- *Penang is not a soup or dry curry it is a thick paste. If too dry, add coconut milk and continue boiling for 3-5 minutes; turn off heat.*

- Add kaffir lime leaf and chilis.
- Serve in a bowl with jasmine rice on the side.

- Simon Wongjanrueang (Grandfather)
  2/1/1935 - 4/16/2020

- Sao Tavilla Wongjanrueang (Grandmother)
  4/2/1940 - 11/19/2024

- Sangat Suwan (Mother) 10/3/1977 - present

- Yut Suwan (Father) 07/29/1973 - present

Thai Basil Chicken Stir Fry

At the tender age of only ten, I found myself in the bustling kitchen of my family home in Thailand, surrounded by the intoxicating aromas of spices and herbs that danced in the air like a well-rehearsed symphony.

My mother, a talented cook, was on a mission that day: to teach me how to make our family's beloved classic *Thai Basil Chicken Stir Fry*. This dish held not just a culinary reputation but also cherished familial memories.

I marveled at how my mother expertly sliced the chicken, the knife gliding seamlessly through the tender meat. "Cooking is not just about feeding people, Annie; it's about creating love," she often reminded me. Those words resonated deep within my heart. I still think back on them often.

As we simmered garlic and chilis in the pan, the rich scent enveloped me like a cozy blanket, wrapping me in warmth and comfort. I watched as she added vibrant basil leaves, transforming the dish into a masterpiece.

Determined to impress my family, I took my lessons seriously. I buried my nose into the fragrant basil leaves, letting their aroma fill my senses, and learned how to balance the flavors of fish sauce and soy sauce to create the perfect stir fry.

Each step felt like a new adventure; every stir of the Wok infused me with growing confidence. By the end of my first day in the kitchen, I could already envision the smiles of my younger brothers and cousins as they eagerly awaited my creation.

The day finally arrived when I decided to surprise my family. With my brothers and cousins gathered around the dinner table, I proudly presented my first-ever *Thai Basil Chicken Stir Fry*.

As I served the dish, my heart raced with anticipation. Gasps of delight echoed off the walls, filling me with immense pride. The fun-loving laughter that surrounded the table was the sweetest melody, affirming my mother's lesson: cooking for loved ones is an act of love that transcends words.

Years later, as fate would have it, I met David Toborowsky.

Our first date was an enchanting evening filled with soft music, warm smiles, and delicious food. I wanted to recreate a slice of my childhood for him, to share a glimpse of my roots. So, I prepared the very same *Thai Basil Chicken Stir Fry* that had once dazzled my family.

As we shared the dish, I watched David's eyes light up with joy, captivated not only by the delicious flavors but by the love that enveloped the meal.

At that moment, I realized that cooking was more than just a skill—it was a bridge connecting my past with my present. The laughter and shared joy around the dinner table echoed the memories of my childhood, now transformed into something new and beautiful with David by my side.

Love filled the air, and I understood that each bite spoke stories of my heritage and the joyous future I envisioned with him, all wrapped beautifully in a simple stir fry.

Thai Basil Chicken Stir Fry

SPICES and SAUCES

1 bunch Thai basil

5-15 Thai chilis - depending on your desired level of spice

1 tablespoon fish sauce

1/4 tablespoon chicken stock, granulated

2 tablespoons oyster sauce

1/2 tablespoon soy sauce

1 tablespoon black soy sauce

avocado or vegetable oil

INGREDIENTS:

1 pound ground chicken

5 cloves peeled garlic

1 medium sliced onion (yellow or white)

1/2 tablespoon brown sugar

DIRECTIONS:

- Chop garlic and chilis together, or moto until minced.
- Peel Thai basil leaf from the stem and set aside.
- Heat Wok or large frying pan, add avacado or vegetable oil.
- Add garlic, onion and chili; mix for 3-4 minutes over medium heat.
- Add ground chicken and mix thoroughly for 5 minutes.
- Lower heat to just under medium.
- Add fish sauce and chicken stock granulated.
- Add sugar, oyster sauce, soy sauce, and black soy sauce.
- Turn heat up to medium and mix together until chicken is cooked.
- Turn off heat and add Thai basil.
- Mix thoroughly, adding spices to your liking.
- Serve with jasmine rice.

Green Curry with Chicken

I stood in the kitchen, a soft smile tugging at my lips as I chopped vibrant vegetables for one of my favorite dishes—*Thai Green Curry with Chicken.*

The kitchen was alive with the intoxicating aroma of fresh basil, the citrusy brightness of lemongrass, and the earthy richness of creamy coconut milk. Each chop of the knife released bursts of fragrance, evoking memories of home in Thailand. I had learned this dish from my mother and was now preparing it for my husband, David.

David, sitting in the living room, could hardly contain his anticipation. The warm, inviting scents wafting from the kitchen hinted at the delicious meal to come. It had been a long day, and I could tell he appreciated the effort I put into crafting this special dish.

We had come so far together since our first meeting on TLC's 90-Day Fiancé, navigating challenges and celebrating our differences. But moments like this—sharing my favorite dishes and connecting with cherished family recipes—always strengthened our bond.

As I stirred the curry in the pot, bubbling sauce filled the air, mingling with the fragrant steam rising from it. I thought about my journey and how far I had come.

When I first moved to America, I deeply missed my family and the vibrant flavors of Thailand. Cooking dishes like this had been my way of holding onto my roots while sharing a piece of myself with David.

With each sprinkle of herbs and every stir of the pot, I felt the warmth of my culture enveloping me as if my mother were there beside me. The green curry's vibrant hue glistened, a testament to the fresh ingredients.

The tender chicken pieces absorbed the aromatic spices, and the thought of David and I enjoying this meal together filled me with joy.

When the curry was finally ready, I brought it to the table, the steam rising like a fragrant invitation. The vibrant green of the curry, the tender chunks of chicken, and the aroma of fresh herbs created a feast for the senses. David's eyes lit up as he took his first bite, the explosion of flavors dancing on his palate made him smile.

"This is incredible," he said, his voice full of admiration and delight.

I smiled, watching David savor the rich, creamy curry, the heat of the spices mingling perfectly with the sweetness of the coconut milk. "I'm so glad you like it," I said, my heart swelling with pride.

At that moment, I felt a deep sense of contentment. It wasn't just the food but the love, the tradition, and the joy of sharing my world with the man I adored. Each bite seemed to weave our stories together, creating a tapestry of flavors, love, and shared memories that would linger long after the last spoonful had been enjoyed.

Green Curry with Chicken

SPICES and SAUCES:

1 bunch Thai basil

3-5 red chilis sliced into small pieces

3.5 tablespoons fish sauce

2.5 tablespoons Thai green curry

Chinese ginger (also known as finger root) sliced into small pieces

INGREDIENTS:

1 pound chicken thighs cut into small pieces

1/2 pound Thai eggplant, diced

1 can coconut milk

2 tablespoons brown or palm sugar

8 kaffir lime leaves

2 cups water

DIRECTIONS:

- Pour half a can of coconut milk into a pot and turn to medium heat.
- Allow it to heat up and stir until the coconut milk is reduced to an oil.
- Add Thai green curry and mix well.
- Add water and Thai eggplant.
- Cook eggplant for 3-5 minutes.
- Add chicken.
- Cook chicken and eggplant for 8-10 minutes.
- Add remaining coconut milk, fish sauce and brown or palm sugar.
- Mix well and cook until chicken is cooked and eggplant is soft.
- Turn off heat and add the sliced Chinese ginger, kaffir lime leaf, Thai basil, and sliced Thai chilis (adjust to spice level) mixing thoroughly.
- Serve with jasmine rice on the side.

Note: adjust the taste to add flavors

Chicken with Lemongrass

I have always been proud of my cooking skills. Raised in Thailand, my culinary talents were an integral part of my identity. I was no stranger to making flavorful dishes. Still, when I moved to Weifang, Shandong Province, to be with my husband, David, I realized that my cooking would have to transcend the familiar spices of home and blend with the flavors of a new culture.

David had been living in China for years as an English teacher, and while he loved the local cuisine, I knew that food was essential to bridging the gap between our worlds. I wanted to give him a taste of home, something that would make him feel connected to my culture.

I decided to make my famous *Thai Fried Chicken* with a twist —a touch of lemongrass, a flavor I knew would surprise and delight him.

The recipe was one my mother had taught me. I had watched as she expertly marinated the chicken in a mixture of garlic, fish sauce, and fresh herbs. This time, I added a special ingredient: fresh lemongrass. The citrusy, fragrant herb reminded me of home. I thought infusing the chicken with a refreshing, aromatic touch would be perfect.

As I carefully prepared the dish in our tiny kitchen, the sizzle of the chicken filled the room. I thought about David, his days spent teaching English to curious students, and how much I appreciated his patience and understanding as I navigated this new life. Cooking was my way of showing love and care, and I wanted my food to remind him of the bond we shared.

When the chicken was golden and crispy, I set the table. After a long day at work, David walked in and immediately smiled at the aroma filling the room. He had missed Thai food, and though the local cuisine in Weifang was good, there was something special about the flavors from my home.

"Smells amazing," he said, sitting down. As he took his first bite, his eyes widened. The lemongrass gave the chicken a bright, tangy kick that he hadn't expected, and it was unlike anything he had tasted before. It was the perfect blend of Thai influences, even in China.

"That's the taste of home," David said, his voice soft with appreciation.

I smiled, feeling a warm sense of pride. I had done more than make a meal; I had brought a piece of my heart to Weifang. Through food, I found a way to connect with David and make our new life together a little sweeter.

Chicken with Lemongrass

SPICES and SAUCES:

chilis (as desired)

2 tablespoons fish sauce

1 teaspoon sugar

1/2 teaspoon black pepper

INGREDIENTS:

1 pound chicken thighs, cut into bite-sized bits

1/2 clove peeled garlic

2 stalks lemongrass

4 tablespoons all-purpose flour

4 tablespoons corn starch

8 tablespoons water

cooking oil for deep frying (vegetable)

DIRECTIONS:

- Chop garlic and lemongrass into small pieces and add chilis if desired.
- Moto the pieces into a fine mixture.
- Clean and cut chicken into 1 to 1.5 inch pieces.
- Mix the sugar, fish sauce, black pepper, and the mixture of lemongrass and garlic into chicken.
- Marinate for at least thirty minutes.
- Add flour, corn starch, and water.
- Mix well into the chicken and marinade for another fifteen minutes.
- Heat Wok or large frying pan to just above medium and add oil for deep frying.
- Add chicken to hot oil and cook.
- Remove chicken when thoroughly cooked and tap dry.
- Serve with favorite dipping sauce.

Laab Chicken – Country Style

With a deep connection to my Thai heritage, I have always been fascinated by the flavors of Issan, the northeastern region of Thailand. Growing up, I would watch my mom, a warm and patient woman, prepare dishes that smelled like home: the sizzling of herbs and spices, the rich flavors mingling in the air. But there was one dish that truly captured my heart: laab, a spicy, tangy minced meat salad that was my mom's signature dish. It was more than just food; it was an expression of love, tradition, and family.

One summer afternoon, as the sun cast a golden hue through our kitchen window, I decided it was time to learn how to make *Laab Chicken*—the very dish that my mom had perfected over the years. Her big smile was warm and encouraging, and she was pleased by my request.

"It's all about balance," she said, setting the ingredients on the counter: chicken breast, lime, chili, mint, cilantro, and, of course, the essential toasted rice powder.

As my mom demonstrated each step, I followed closely, feeling a wave of nostalgia wash over me. Her hands moved with grace and confidence, chopping the chicken into small, even pieces, making sure to preserve the tenderness of the meat. She taught me how to toast the rice, watching it transform into a golden, fragrant powder that would give the laab its signature texture. The smell of the toasting rice wafted through the kitchen, instantly transporting me back to my childhood. But the real lesson was in the seasoning.

"This is where the magic happens," my mom said, gently adding fish sauce, lime juice, and a touch of sugar to balance the heat with the chilis.

I watched closely, learning to adjust the flavors by tasting and adding a bit more, a dash of this, a pinch of that. The mixture of spicy, sour, and savory became more than just ingredients—it was the essence of family, passed down from generation to generation.

When the laab was finally ready, I felt a deep sense of pride swell within me. The dish wasn't just a recipe; it was a piece of my mother's heart, and now it was mine to carry forward.

As we sat together, savoring the dish, I realized that it wasn't just the cooking that connected me to my roots but the love, patience, and memories my mom had shared with me. Each bite was a reminder of our shared history, the laughter echoing through the kitchen, and the lessons learned at her side.

In that moment, I understood that laab is a common dish served in Thailand, but my mom's laab is like no other. It can't be found in a small shop or a high-end restaurant; it exists only in her kitchen, crafted with care and infused with love.

This experience solidified our bond, a treasure I will hold close to my heart forever, a connection that transcends time and space. Laab, with all its vibrant flavors, had become a bridge linking my past to my present, a celebration of my heritage that I will continue to honor for years to come.

Laab Chicken - Country Style

SPICES and SAUCES:

1 tablespoon chili powder

1 teaspoon salt

1/4 bunch cilantro

1 teaspoon MSG (optional)

1 tablespoon fish sauce

INGREDIENTS:

1/2 pound ground chicken

1/2 a red onion

1 clove garlic - peeled

1/2 bunch green onion

2 limes

2 tablespoons sticky or sweet rice

3 tablespoons cooking oil

DIRECTIONS:

- Turn heat to medium; add sticky rice or sweet rice to roast in Wok.
- Stir rice continually until golden brown.
- Turn off heat and turn the rice into a powder by motoing or grounding it.
- Moto garlic and set aside.
- Return heat to medium and add cooking oil to Wok.
- Add garlic (do not let garlic burn).
- Add ground chicken.
- Mix until chicken is cooked; turn off heat.
- Move chicken and garlic to a mixing bowl.
- Add salt, fish sauce, MSG, rice powder, and chili powder.
- Add chopped red onion, cilantro, and green onion.
- Squeeze limes into the mixture and taste; add more as needed.
- Serve on a plate, adding sliced cucumbers, lettuce and cilantro as garnish.

Chicken Soup with Tomato & Potato

I often find myself reminiscing about my childhood in Thailand, particularly the simple yet comforting moments that filled my heart with joy. One memory that stands out vividly is from my school days when lunchtime meant looking forward to a special treat: *Chicken Soup with Tomatoes and Potatoes.*

It wasn't just an ordinary lunch; this dish symbolized warmth, care, and the love that enveloped my family. My school occasionally served this comforting soup; when it appeared on the menu, it felt like a celebration. The savory aroma of tender chicken simmering in a rich, fragrant broth filled with soft potatoes and juicy tomatoes wafted through the air, mingling with hints of garlic and herbs. It was impossible to ignore. It wasn't a fancy meal, but it felt like a luxury, a delicious taste of home that wrapped around me like a warm blanket.

The soup was served in a bowl just the right size, with a ladle that scooped up a perfect portion. The warm, inviting liquid swirled around the potatoes and tender chunks of chicken. The steam from the bowl danced in the air, carrying the mouthwatering scents into my eager nostrils. It always came with a fluffy scoop of rice on the side, which I would mix into the soup, creating a comforting, hearty combination that filled me with satisfaction.

The simplicity of the dish made it even more special; something about the balance of flavors—the sweetness of the ripe tomatoes, the earthiness of the soft potatoes, and the savory goodness of the chicken—made it taste like a hug in a bowl.

I remember how, even as a young child, I eagerly looked forward to the days when this delightful meal appeared on the school lunch menu. It wasn't just about the food but the feeling of being cared for and cherished.

The soup reminded me of my mother's nurturing hands, who often cooked similar meals at home, filling our kitchen with warmth and love. It evoked feelings of family, tradition, and the joy that simple things could bring.

Now, as an adult, I find myself recreating this comforting dish in my own kitchen. The familiar scents wafting through the air transport me back to those cherished moments.

Though the ingredients might be slightly different, the essence of the meal remains the same—something to warm the soul and bring comfort. The rich aroma fills my home whenever I serve it to my loved ones. I share the story of my school lunch memory, knowing that food, like love, has the profound power to connect us to our past and each other.

Chicken Soup with Tomato and Potato will always be more than just a meal; it's a beautiful memory of my childhood and the enduring love that shaped me.

Chicken Soup with Tomato & Potato

SPICES and SAUCES:

3 pieces garlic, minced

2 bouillon cubes chicken stock

1 teaspoon salt

1/2 teaspoon sugar

1 tablespoon oyster sauce (optional)

INGREDIENTS:

1 pound chicken thighs cut into small pieces

3 tomatoes cut into small pieces

3 potatoes cut into small pieces

1 stalk celery cut into small pieces

1/2 white or yellow onion, sliced

1-1.5 litres water

DIRECTIONS:

- In large pot bring water to a boil.
- Add chicken bullion, garlic, onion, tomato, potato, and celery.
- Add salt, sugar, and oyster sauce.
- Let it boil for 10 minutes.
- Add chicken and bring back to boil, removing film from the top.
- After chicken is cooked, reduce temperature and simmer for twenty minutes.
- Serve with jasmine rice (Optional).

A Memory from David

In December 2020, beneath a ceiling of gray clouds and the biting chill of winter, I felt turmoil deep within my heart. Just three weeks had passed since my father's unexpected passing, a loss that turned my world upside down. At the same time, Annie had fallen ill with COVID-19, her vibrant spirit dimmed by the relentless grip of the virus. It broke my heart to watch her struggle, leaving me feeling helpless and heartbroken.

I called my mom for one of her favorite recipes, longing for the warmth of my grandmother and great-grandmother's kitchen. I decided to honor their memory by making their beloved *Matzah Ball Chicken Soup*—a warm dish that had comforted my family for generations. Food has a unique way of healing the soul, and I was determined to bring a taste of love into our home.

Gathering all the ingredients, my hands trembled slightly as I prepared the chicken broth. I recalled just how my great-grandmother taught me to let it simmer slowly, extracting every ounce of flavor. As the aroma filled the kitchen, I could almost hear her voice guiding me, urging me not to rush the process.

Chopping carrots and celery, I envisioned the warmth the soup would bring to Annie, who lay resting in bed. I wanted to get her feeling well again, and I knew this soup would help.

Matzah Ball Chicken Soup

With each matzah ball that I rolled and dropped into the simmering broth, I poured my heart into the dish—my love, my sorrow, and my hopes for brighter days. Finally, after what felt like an eternity, I ladled the steaming soup into a bowl and carried it to Annie, filled with a mix of anticipation and trepidation.

When I placed the steaming bowl in front of her, her tired eyes sparkled with gratitude. She took her first spoonful, and a smile crept across her face.

"This is amazing, David. It feels like a warm hug," she said, her voice soft, yet filled with joy.

At that moment, I felt a flicker of peace amidst the chaos of loss and illness. As we shared that bowl of soup, I realized that love, memories, and tradition were powerful ingredients in our journey together.

We were finding a way to heal through heartache, one spoonful at a time. While this recipe has changed over time—ingredients that were once common in Eastern Europe or Charleston, West Virginia, are different today—the soup remains as delicious and comforting as it was a hundred years ago.

Matzah Ball Chicken Soup

CHICKEN BROTH

SPICES and SAUCES:

dash garlic powder

1 bunch fresh dill, cut into pieces

chicken stock bullion

dash black pepper

INGREDIENTS:

1 whole organic chicken, washed and cleaned

2 stalks celery, cut into small pieces

2 carrots, sliced into small pieces

1 package egg bowtie noodles

DIRECTIONS:

- Wash chicken with Kosher salt, let sit in water for fifteen minutes.
- Fill large pot 3/4 full and bring water to boil.
- Add bullion, pepper, and whole chicken, cooking 3 minutes.
- Decrease heat to simmer.
- Add celery, dill, garlic powder, and carrots.
- Allow chicken to simmer for many hours until it falls off the bone.
- Remove chicken fat skim from top of the water.
- Remove all meat from the bone and return meat to pot - add water as needed.
- Taste soup broth and add chicken stock as desired.
- Cook a few more hours for the broth to absorb the flavors.

Matzah Ball Chicken Soup

MATZAH BALLS

SPICES and SAUCES:

1 teaspoon salt

1 teaspoon black pepper

INGREDIENTS:

3 eggs

3 tablespoons chicken broth

3 tablespoons chicken fat

3/4 cup Matzah meal

DIRECTIONS:

- Whisk eggs. Add chicken broth, salt, pepper.
- Stir in the Matzah meal.
- Add the cold fat and hot soup to melt the cold fat.
- Mix well.
- Refrigerate for several hours, or overnight.
- Remove from refrigerator and roll into 1-inch balls (grease or moisten hands to avoid sticking)
- In a separate pot with boiling water and a dash of salt, add Matzah balls.
- Cover and cook for twenty minutes.
- When cooked, use fork to poke holes in Matzah balls and add to chicken soup.
- Cook until the Matzah balls float to the top.
- Add noodles and let sit for 10 minutes.
- Serve in a bowl with or with out crackers.

** my grandmother loved to add black pepper.

David's love of good food came from his mother, grandmother and great-grandmother. They all spent countless hours together, mastering the skills of cooking.

Linda Borstein Toborowsky
Mother:
November 22, 1942-Current

Pauline Ostrin Borstein
Grandmother:
March 7, 1914-December 26, 2000

Eve Compinsky Ostrin
Great-Grandmother:
1893-1969

Murray Toborowsky
Father:
October 20, 1940-December 04, 2020

Murray and Linda's Wedding Photo

DISHES WITH
Vegetables

Papaya Salad

Life unfolded simply in a small village near the border of Laos in Thailand. Sweet memories of those sun-drenched afternoons, when the golden light cast a warm hue over the lush fields of the Isaan region, still fill me with a deep sense of nostalgia. Our home was always alive with the rich aroma of my grandmother's cooking.

Grandmother was the heart and soul of our family, a woman whose wisdom and warmth were woven into the fabric of our village. Each day, she would gather us around the wooden table in our open-air kitchen, where the breeze from the Mekong River mingled with savory scents of her dishes. Her specialty was *Spicy Papaya Salad*—more than food, it was part of our identity.

Papayas grew abundantly in Isaan, dotting our garden and the fields surrounding us. They were as common as wildflowers and as treasured as Grandma's stories. Her *Spicy Papaya Salad*, a dish that was more than just a meal, but a symbol of our family's unity and love, was a testament to the significance of family recipes.

I remember standing beside her, my small hands eager to learn as she guided me through the process of making the salad. The papaya, firm and green, was sliced into thin strips, each slice echoing in the quiet kitchen. The pestle and the mortar was used to crush garlic, chilis, and lime, releasing their strong aromas.

Each ingredient came alive under her careful touch. The vibrant flavors blended together like the colors of a sunset, with sugar and fish sauce creating a harmony that echoed the love in our family.

This simple recipe became a comforting staple of our lives, a testament to resilience and joy. It reminded us that even during times of scarcity, the earth provided, and the warmth of family transformed every meal into a celebration.

As I grew older and moved far from those sunlit fields, every bite of that *Spicy Papaya Salad* transported me back to our kitchen, and my grandmother, to the laughter and wisdom that flowed as freely as the river outside.

Years later, as I stand in my own kitchen, far removed from my childhood's sights and sounds, I often long for those moments. As I gather the ingredients—papayas, garlic, chilis—and begin to prepare the salad now, memories flood back with each slice and mash: Grandma's laughter, gentle guidance, and the love that infused every dish she created.

The familiar flavors burst in my mouth as I take the first bite, and tears fill my eyes. It's as if she is right there with me, her spirit enveloping me in a warm embrace. At this moment, I realize that food is more than sustenance; it carries our memories, love, and heritage.

Spicy papaya Salad is not merely a dish; it is a bridge to my past, a reminder of home, and a celebration of the bond that connects me to my grandmother and the land we cherish.

No matter where life takes me, her love will always be a part of me, seasoning my life with the richness of our shared history.

Papaya Salad

SPICES and SAUCES:

2 tablespoons fish sauce

MSG (optional)

1 tablespoon fermented fish paste (Optional)

INGREDIENTS:

1 green papaya, grated

3-5 cherry tomatoes

2 tablespoons palm sugar (Brown)

1-2 limes

3 long green beans, cut into 1 inch pieces

5 chilis (less for non-spicy more for spicier)

garlic 2-3 cloves, peeled

DIRECTIONS:

- Add 2 handfuls of grated papaya into a big bowl.
- Add cherry tomatoes, garlic, green bean pieces, and palm or brown sugar.
- Add fish sauce, limes, and fermented fish paste.
- Moto chilis, garlic, green beans, and add to papaya mixture.
- And all sauces, mixing thoroughly.
- Add any ingredients to achieve desired taste.

In the sun-soaked plains of Isaan, where laughter danced on the breeze, and the distant call of the market filled the air, our childhood was a vibrant celebration of flavors that defined our culture. Our family gathered around the table each day, and at its heart lay a heaping bowl of *Som Tom*—papaya salad. A delightful debate brewed within this beloved dish: Laotian or Thai?

Laotian *Som Tom* was the lifeblood of our home. It was crafted with the freshest green papaya, fragrant garlic, and a generous spoonful of fermented fish paste. My parents would rhythmically pound the ingredients in a mortar, the sound echoing like a heartbeat through our kitchen, infusing the air with a rich aroma that spoke of tradition.

However, while that pungent scent wrapped around my elders like a warm embrace, it often left my siblings and me wrinkling our noses in hesitation. The earthy smell of fish paste was a comfort for them, but for us children, it was a flavor we struggled to understand and tried to avoid.

On our more rebellious days, we would plead for the Thai version—a sweet and sour delight that sparkled with lime juice and palm sugar. This dish danced on our tongues, a refreshing burst of flavors that sang of summer days and carefree laughter.

The crispness of the Thai *Som Tom* contrasted sharply with the deeper, funkier notes of its Laotian counterpart, captivating our youthful hearts.

As children, we reveled in the thrill of the sweet and tangy, enchanted by the balance of flavors that made our taste buds tingle. Yet, there was an unspoken understanding that our culinary journey was just beginning.

With each passing year, our palates evolved; we gradually learned to appreciate the complexity of the Laotian style. We discovered that every whiff of fish paste was steeped in stories of tradition, family gatherings, and the love that infused our meals.

Now, as I reminisce, I recognize that both versions of *Som Tom* were far more than mere food; they were threads woven into the rich tapestry of our childhood. Each bite carried the essence of home, a connection to our roots, and the simple joys of growing up in Isaan. The vibrancy of those gatherings—filled with laughter, spirited debates over the best *Som Tom,* and the warmth of family—served as the backdrop to our lives.

Ultimately, it was not just about the flavors that graced our palates but the memories we forged around them. *Som Tom* became a symbol of our journey, encapsulating the love and tradition that nourished us and bound us together as we savored the past while embracing the future.

Today, as I prepare this beloved dish in my own kitchen, I carry forward the legacy of both styles, knowing that with each bite, I honor the laughter, the love, and the beauty of our shared history.

Som Tom Thai

SPICES and SAUCES:

1 tablespoon fish sauce

INGREDIENTS:

1 green papaya, shredded into 2 bunches

3-5 chilis

2 cloves garlic, peeled

1/2 tablespoon lime juice

3-4 long green beans, cut into 1-inch pieces

1/2 tablespoon palm sugar

4 cherry tomatos

ground peanuts (Optional)

2-3 carrots, shredded

DIRECTIONS:

- Shred green papaya and carrots, set aside.
- Mix garlic, chilis, and green beans in moto; use pestle to mash into small pieces.
- Add fish sauce, palm sugar, cherry tomatoes, ground peanuts, and lime juice.
- Add shredded carrots and papaya.
- Mix together and enjoy.

Fried Spring Rolls

I sat quietly beside my grandmother, our hands brushing against the cool bamboo of our small village home in Som Sanuk. The sun was low, casting a warm golden hue over the rice paddies, sprawling out like a beautiful quilt.

The gentle rustle of the leaves and the distant chirping of crickets wrapped around us, making the moment feel special. With her silver hair neatly tucked into a bun, my grandmother turned to me with a smile that felt like a precious secret just for us.

"Pak Khat," she said, her voice steady but full of excitement. "We go to Pak Khat. The market is there. Fried spring rolls, the best in all the land!"

My heart fluttered at the thought of Pak Khat. I had grown up listening to her stories about this bustling town, a lively place not far from our village. Today, it was finally my turn to see it for myself.

We set off, walking down the dusty road. The sun was dipping lower, casting long shadows behind us. The rhythm of our steps matched the soft hum of the evening breeze, whispering secrets of the land. It was enchanting.

Our path led us through bright green fields, past homes with thatched roofs, where laughter and the scent of cooking drifted from open windows. With each step, my excitement grew, the air thick with the promise of adventure.

When we finally hopped onto the back of an old pick-up truck, I felt the thrill of embarking on an adventure away from our quiet village.

The truck rattled along the bumpy road, and I leaned into my grandmother, her warmth grounding me as we bounced along. I could hear the town's distant hum growing louder, like a heartbeat quickening in my chest.

As we arrived at the market in Pak Khat, my eyes widened, taking in the colors and sounds. The crispy, golden spring rolls gleamed under the bright sun, calling to me like a treasure. My grandmother handed over a small pouch of Thai baht, and in return, received a warm bundle of those fried delights, the aroma teasing my senses like a caress.

We found a weathered bench to sit on, the perfect spot to enjoy our treats. My grandmother carefully wrapped the spring rolls in crisp lettuce leaves, her hands steady and practiced. She offered one to me with a proud smile, and I took a bite. The crunch of the lettuce, the rich, savory filling of the spring rolls, and the laughter bubbling between us created a symphony of joy.

In that simple, quiet moment, surrounded by the buzz of the market, I felt a deep connection to my roots—the love of a grandmother who knew how to turn even the simplest pleasures into cherished memories.

As we sat there, my grandmother's stories came alive in my heart. I realized that in Pak Khat, with spring rolls in hand, I had found something timeless—an essence of home that would stay with me, no matter where life would take me. The laughter, the scents, and the warmth of her presence were now woven into the fabric of my being, a reminder that the greatest treasures are often found in the simplest moments shared with those we love.

Fried Spring Rolls

SPICES and SAUCES:

1/2 clove minced garlic

2 tablespoons oyster sauce

3 tablespoons light soy sauce

1/2 teaspoon granulated chicken stock

1/2 teaspoon sugar

1/2 teaspoon black pepper

2 tablespoons cooking oil

INGREDIENTS:

1 package spring roll wraps

1 egg

1/4 pound ground pork

1/4 pound minced shrimp

1 carrot, finely chopped

1 handful cabbage, finely chopped

5 shitake mushrooms, minced

2-3 carrots, fincly chopped

peanuts (Optional)

1 bunch glass noodles, chopped into pieces

1/2 head Napa lettuce

DIRECTIONS:

- Heat Wok or large fry pan on medium, add oil.
- Add minced garlic, followed by pork and shrimp.
- Mix for 1 minute. Add all vegetables, glass noodles, spices and sauces. Mix.
- Remove mixture from pan and let cool.
- Whisk egg in separate bowl.
- Take 1 wrap and lay flat. Add 2 tablespoons mixture and drop in center of wrap.
- Fold wrap like an envelope from bottom, tuck sides in and dip a small bit of egg to seal wrap. Repeat until all wraps are filled.
- Add oil for deep frying, turn to medium heat. When oil is hot, add spring rolls.
- Flip once, browning both sides of spring roll.
- Remove and place on plate with paper towel to absorb oil.
- Cut in pieces to cool. Serve with lettuce wraps and sweet and sour dipping sauce.

When Annie contracted Covid-19, David made her his special Matzah Ball Soup. (recipe found on page 52)

Grandfather's Stuffed Mushrooms

In the heart of Thailand's rainy season, the countryside transforms into a lush paradise draped in vibrant greens from May to October. The rain falls in a soothing cascade, creating a gentle melody that dances across the land. During this magical time, my grandfather and I would embark on our beloved ritual of foraging for wild mushrooms.

Armed with a small bamboo basket that my grandfather lovingly wove for me, I would venture into the dewy undergrowth, my senses heightened by the world around me. The rich, earthy aroma of the forest floor mingled with the fresh, invigorating scent of rain-soaked leaves. Each step was accompanied by the soft patter of raindrops and the occasional rustle of creatures hidden among the ferns. My heart swelled with excitement, eager to uncover the hidden treasures peeking out from beneath the damp foliage.

Once we returned home, the real magic began. With his weathered hands, which had known the land for decades, my grandfather would prepare our harvest for a special treat. He carefully sliced the mushrooms, their tender flesh glistening in the light. These mushrooms, a product of our shared adventure in the rain, were the heart of our family tradition. Finely chopped lemongrass added a refreshing, citrusy note, while a few fiery chilis brought a gentle kick. Just a pinch of salt was all he needed to enhance the flavors; its simplicity was a testament to his wisdom.

He wrapped the seasoned mushrooms in banana leaves, their vibrant green hue strikingly contrasting the earthy tones of the mushrooms. With a practiced hand, he secured the parcels with twine and hung them on a skewer over an open fire.

The flames danced beneath, crackling as they licked the banana leaves, infusing the mushrooms with a subtle, smoky aroma that filled the air and wrapped around us.

As the mushrooms sizzled over the fire, the kitchen filled with a tantalizing scent—smoky, citrusy, and slightly spicy—a symphony that made my mouth water. We collected around the fire, our laughter mixing with the sound of rain drumming on the roof, anticipating the moment when my grandfather would unveil the banana leaves. When he did, steam rose like a fragrant cloud, revealing the perfectly cooked mushrooms, glistening and inviting.

Each bite was a comforting blend of flavors, the lemongrass and chilis harmonizing beautifully with the earthiness of the mushrooms. In those rainy season days, amidst the drumming rain and the crackle of the fire, everything felt just right. The food's warmth and the joy of sharing it with my grandfather transformed every stormy day into a cherished memory, wrapping us in a cozy cocoon of love and tradition.

As we sat together, the world outside faded away, replaced by the simple pleasure of our shared meal. In those moments, I felt a deep connection to my roots, the love flowing between us like the river that nourished our land.

Those days, filled with mushrooms and laughter, became the heart of my childhood—forever etched in my memory, a reminder of the beauty found in nature and the bonds of family.

Grandfather's Stuffed Mushrooms

INGREDIENTS:

any type of fresh or packaged mushrooms

1 bunch lemongrass

1-2 chilis (depending on spice level)

salt to taste

DIRECTIONS:

- Wash and slice 1 package of mushrooms.
- Cut lemongrass into small pieces.
- Chop chilis (as many as you desire).
- Bring 1/4 cup water to boil.
- Add lemongrass, mushrooms, and chilis to boiling water.
- Season with salt as needed.
- Cook until mushrooms are fully cooked.
- Serve and enjoy.

Kai jiao

Honestly, I can't remember exactly when I first started making *Kai jiao*. Still, I know it was the very first recipe and dish I ever put on my personal menu.

Back then, eggs were incredibly cheap—two for five baht or four for ten baht. That's roughly about thirty cents for four! It was such a delightful treat, especially for a young girl like me.

Sometimes, when we could get away with it, we would sneak chicken eggs from my dad's farm. We raised those chickens for meat rather than their eggs, so they were a bit different but absolutely delicious.

Kai jiao was perfect for breakfast because it was quick to make, saving us precious time before we headed off to school, and it filled us up nicely.

To make it, I'd start by heating some cooking oil in the pan. Then, I would mix the eggs with fish sauce, minced garlic, and a little sugar. Back then, that was it—no soy sauce or oyster sauce. I had no idea those sauces existed, and we didn't have them at home; they were simply too expensive.

Sometimes, I'd even throw in a pinch of MSG to enhance the flavor, which made it delicious.

When you woke up feeling hungry in the mornings, *Kai jiao* was just what you wanted. You'd eat it with sticky rice, of course, which made the meal even more satisfying.

So here's how you make it.

Heat four tablespoons of cooking oil in the pan, mix four eggs in a bowl with about a tablespoon of fish sauce, a quarter spoon of sugar, a pinch of MSG, and some crushed garlic. Mix it all together thoroughly and basically, that's it!

After mixing everything together, I would pour the egg mixture into the hot oil. It would cook quickly, and I'd flip it over to finish cooking. The outside would be crispy and golden, while the inside remained soft and fluffy. For four eggs, I'd use about four tablespoons of oil—after all, we loved the extra oil, especially with rice, which added an extra layer of flavor.

After breakfast, I'd pack some *Kai jiao* for school, and during lunchtime, my friends and I would gather and compare our lunches. It was funny—there would be seven of us, and we all had *Kai jiao*! It was so easy to make, which made it perfect for everyone to enjoy and share.

It was a simple dish, but back then, it felt like I was dining in a five-star hotel, savoring every bite.

Today, whenever I make *Kai jiao*, each bite brings me right back to the memories of carefree mornings and the simple joys of friendship.

Kai jiao

SPICES and SAUCES:

4 tablespoons cooking oil

2 pieces garlic-minced

1 tablespoon fish sauce

pinch of salt or MSG

INGREDIENTS:

4 eggs (Organic Brown is Best)

DIRECTIONS:

- Heat oil in pan.
- Whisk eggs in a bowl and add the minced garlic, fish sauce, and MSG.
- Mix in well and add into the pan after the oil heats up.
- Flip over and cook to liking.

Cauliflower with Egg

Growing up in Isaan, the flavors around me were as vibrant as the sun-drenched fields that framed our home. With their limited resources, my family didn't just cook; but we transformed our humble surroundings into a culinary paradise, harnessing seasonal ingredients and spices to create meals that transcended mere sustenance—they were cherished memories.

As children, my siblings and I often turned our noses up at certain vegetables, with cauliflower topping the list. Its pale, firm texture seemed uninviting to our youthful appetites. Yet, my grandmother possessed a magical ability to transform this humble vegetable into something utterly irresistible. With a twinkle in her eye, she would venture into our garden, harvest the freshest cauliflower, and chop it finely, infusing it with love and creativity.

In her kitchen, she would crack golden, fresh eggs into a bowl, whisking them with a gentle touch, adding a pinch of salt and a dash of pepper. Then came her secret—a sprinkle of fish sauce, a hint of soy sauce, and sometimes turmeric for a splash of color.

As the mixture hit the pan, the sound of the eggs sizzling, the sight of the cauliflower turning golden, and the intoxicating aroma filling our home, wrapping us in warmth like a beloved embrace, we could hardly wait to get a taste.

Her cauliflower dish became a treasured staple, whether served for breakfast or dinner. Each bite was a revelation—a delightful contrast of crunchy, soft, salty, and savory, weaving a tapestry of flavors that made us eagerly anticipate our meals. The once-dreaded, pale vegetable transformed into a comfort food that we couldn't get enough of.

As we matured, we came to appreciate the simplicity and brilliance behind our grandmother's creations. Her meals were not merely about nourishment; they were lessons in resourcefulness, tradition, and the profound love that binds family together. This tradition, passed down through generations, is a thread that connects us to our past and shapes our present.

Even now, the taste of her cauliflower dish evokes a flood of memories—family gatherings filled with laughter, the aroma of home-cooked meals, and the flavors that shaped our childhood. It's a reminder that food is not just sustenance but a source of comfort and joy.

In each mouthful, I can still feel the warmth of her kitchen and hear the echoes of our joyful chatter. Her cooking was a celebration of life, a reminder that even the most unassuming ingredients could bring us together.

Today, as I recreate her dish, I carry her legacy forward, transforming simple moments into lasting memories, just as she did. In this way, her spirit lives on, reminding me that love, creativity, and a touch of magic can turn the ordinary into the extraordinary.

Cauliflower with Egg

SPICES and SAUCES:

1 dash of fish Sauce

dash of salt and pepper

3 cloves peeled garlic

dash of chili powder

2 green onions, chopped into pieces

1/2 tablespoon chicken stock, granulated

1/2 tablespoons soy sauce

1 tablespoon oyster sauce

INGREDIENTS:

1/2 head of cauliflower

4 eggs

1/4 tablespoon sugar

Note: Bacon can be added as an option

DIRECTIONS:

- Wash and chop cauliflower into small pieces.
- Crush garlic and chop the onions and chilis.
- Heat Wok or large frying pan with 4 tablespoons of oil over medium heat.
- Add garlic and chilis - stir for 10-15 seconds.
- Add cauliflower and stir 3 minutes.
- Add eggs into cauliflower.
- Add chicken stock granulated, soy sauce, sugar, oyster sauce, salt, pepper, and fish sauce.
- Mix thoroughly until cooked.
- Turn off heat.
- Top with green onion.
- Serve with jasmine rice.

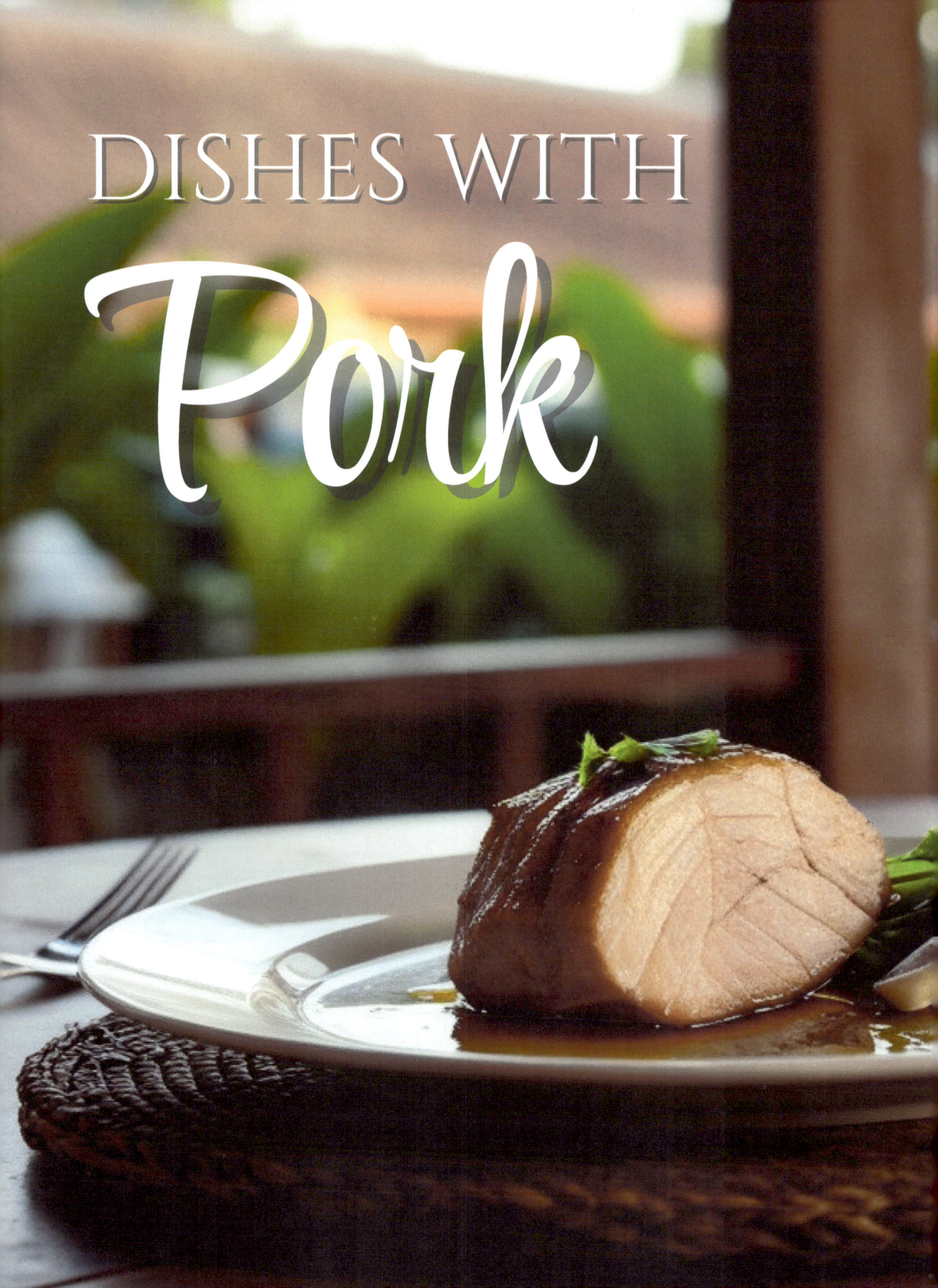

DISHES WITH
Pork

Khao Tom (Rice Soup)

On a chilly winter afternoon, I moved about our snug little apartment in China, a warm haven against the cold outside. Snowflakes fluttered from the sky, each one a fleeting miracle that melted away a little too soon. As I stirred the bubbling pot on the stove, the familiar scents of my cooking began to fill the air, creating an anticipation for the comforting meal that was about to be served.

I could hear David's footsteps approaching, drawn in by the aroma of my famous *Thai Rice Soup* with pork bones. "Come lend a hand!" I called, turning to greet him with a smile that I hoped would brighten his day. His presence always warms my heart, even on the coldest days, and I love sharing the kitchen with him.

He joined me in the kitchen, peeling garlic and ginger while I stirred the pot. "This soup is the perfect cure for a cold day," I said, watching his spirits lift with each moment spent together. As we worked side by side, I felt a sense of camaraderie that made the process even more enjoyable. Cooking has a way of bringing us closer, transforming the simple act of preparing a meal into a cherished ritual.

As I shared some stories from my childhood in Thailand, I recounted the evenings spent in my mother's kitchen, where the air was thick with the aroma of spices and laughter. I told him about the vibrant markets filled with fresh ingredients and the way my mother's hands danced as she skillfully prepared our family meals. With each story, I could see the distance from his home fade in his eyes, replaced by the warmth of our shared experience and the joy of our connection.

With every ingredient I added—fish sauce, fresh herbs, and a sprinkle of chili flakes—I felt the kitchen come alive, filled with the promise of a comforting meal. David chimed in with his own memories of cooking with his family, the lessons learned, and the laughs shared over spilled flour and burnt edges. It was such a delightful exchange, weaving our backgrounds together into a tapestry of flavors and warmth.

Soon enough, we sat at our little table with steaming bowls before us, the soup glistening in the soft light of our cozy dining nook. The first sip took me back to those sun-drenched afternoons of my childhood, where the savory broth, tender pork, and soft rice blended together in a way that felt like an embrace. I watched as David savored each bite, his eyes closing in delight, and my heart swelled with joy.

"This is incredible, Annie!" he exclaimed after his first taste, and I couldn't help but smile wider. We laughed and talked, the soup's warmth and connection melting away the winter chill outside. Every spoonful was an invitation to share more stories, to dream about future meals we would create together, and to savor the joy of our little rituals.

At that moment, I knew that home wasn't just a place; it was wherever we were together, sharing love and a hearty meal, creating our little world filled with comfort and joy. As the snow continued to fall outside, we felt cocooned in our own bubble of warmth, laughter, and the delicious reminder that no matter how cold the world might be, our kitchen would always be a warm and inviting sanctuary.

Khao Tom (Rice Soup)

SPICES and SAUCES:

1/2 tablespoon salt and pepper to taste

1 bunch cilantro

1 tablespoon soy sauce

2 tablespoons oyster sauce

chili flakes (optional)

INGREDIENTS:

2 cups cooked jasmine rice

1/2 pound pork bones or small pork ribs (can use ground chicken as substitute)

1 green oinion, chopped

5 pieces garlic, peeled

1.5 liters water

2 tablespoons granulated chicken stock

1/2 tablespoon sugar

DIRECTIONS:

- In a large pot, bring water and salt to boil.
- Mince the garlic.
- Add pork bones or ribs and adjust temperature to medium heat.
- Allow the pork bones to cook with garlic and salt until tender (15-20 min) add water as necessary.
- Add rice, chicken stock, sugar, soy sauce, and oyster sauce.
- Cook on medium for 5 minutes.
- Reduce heat to low.
- Taste and adjust flavors according to your liking.
- Serve in soup bowls.
- Add cilantro, green onion, black pepper, and spicy chili flakes.
- Serve and enjoy.

Issan Sausages

I had always admired how my Aunt Nin and Uncle Tepp ran their little street food stand in our village in Buneg Kan, Thailand. The air was filled with the irresistible scent of grilled meats, mingling with the sweet aroma of jasmine rice and the zesty notes of fresh herbs. Locals swarmed to buy their famous *Issan Sausages*, each bite bursting with flavor and tradition. Growing up in a small, humble home, I had never learned how to make the sausages myself, but today, my aunt and uncle had promised to teach me.

"Annie, today you'll learn the secret of our sausages," Aunt Nin said, her eyes twinkling with warmth and excitement. "But remember, it's not just about the ingredients. It's about the love you put into it." Her words hung in the air like a gentle reminder of the heart behind every dish.

I nodded eagerly, my stomach growling at the thought of those mouthwatering sausages sizzling on the grill. Uncle Tepp handed me a large mixing bowl, the contents already laid out before me—minced pork, fragrant jasmine rice, minced garlic, fresh lemongrass, and a few secret spices they wouldn't even whisper to me. The vibrant colors and textures promised a feast for the senses.

"Mix it by hand, Annie," Uncle Tepp instructed, giving me a gentle but firm look. "This is how you make the flavor stick." As I dug my hands into the raw mixture, the scents of garlic and lemongrass filled the air, enveloping me like a sunny day. It felt foreign, yet comforting, as if the village itself had been waiting for me to join in this age-old tradition.

The mixture was cool and slightly sticky, and with each knead, I could feel the flavors melding together. Once the meat was well-mixed, Aunt Nin showed me how to stuff it into the casings, twisting each sausage tightly to create perfectly plump forms.

I struggled at first; the mixture slipped through my fingers, but with my aunt's patient guidance, I finally got the hang of it. I laughed when a sausage burst open, spilling rice everywhere, but Aunt Nin simply patted my shoulder.

"Don't worry. Even the best make mistakes," she said with a wink, her laughter ringing like a melody.

As we grilled the sausages over an open flame that afternoon, the sizzle of the meat mingled with the crackle of the fire, creating a symphony of sounds that made my mouth water. The aroma wafted through the air, drawing curious neighbors closer, their eyes lighting up at the familiar scent. I felt a deep connection to my heritage, the flavors of my childhood coming alive in a way I had never anticipated.

As the sausages cooked, Aunt Nin prepared a dipping sauce with a vibrant blend of fish sauce, lime juice, and chili flakes, a tangy complement to the richness of the grilled meat. "This is what brings the dish together," she explained, pouring the sauce into a small bowl. "Each bite should dance on your tongue."

Finally, the sausages were ready. They gleamed under the sun, their golden-brown skins promising a burst of flavor inside. I took my first bite, and the world around me melted away. The smoky, savory goodness of the meat, combined with the fragrant herbs, all perfectly balanced by the zing of the dipping sauce. It was a taste of home, a celebration of my roots, and in that moment, I felt a profound sense of belonging and joy.

Issan Sausages

SPICES and SAUCES:

1 teaspoon granulated chicken stock

2 teaspoons sugar

2 teaspoons salt

2 cloves garlic

1 teaspoon ground black pepper

1 teaspoon cilantro

INGREDIENTS:

1/2 pound of ground pork

3 cups cooked jasmine rice, cooled

1 stalk of lemongrass, sliced into small pieces

1 package normal sized hog casings

cooking string

DIRECTIONS:

- Cook jasmine rice and let sit until cold.
- Moto the garlic and lemongrass until thoroughly mixed.
- Add pork, garlic and lemongrass mixture to large mixing bowl.
- Add cooked rice, chicken stock, sugar, salt, garlic, pepper, and cilantro.
- Mix thoroughly.
- Using a sausage maker, stuff casings with mixture and create 1-inch sausages.
- Tie off with cooking string.
- Cook in air fryer on high for 8 minutes each side or until well cooked well.
- If using a grill, cook until meat is bursting.
- Serve with fresh ginger and cucumber slices.

Pumpkin Red Curry

I stood in the cozy kitchen of my Arizona home, the warm sun casting her usual soft glow through the windows. I was preparing something I never thought I'd come to love— *Pumpkin Red Curry* with pork. As I chopped the vibrant vegetables, the sweet, earthy scent of fresh pumpkin mingled with the sharpness of garlic and the aromatic notes of ginger, transporting my mind back to my childhood in Thailand.

Back then, this dish had been one of my least favorites; the earthy sweetness of pumpkin, combined with the bold spiciness of red curry, had felt overwhelming to my young palate. I would always push it aside at the dinner table, hoping my mom would let me have something else.

But today was different. I had grown to appreciate the complex flavors of my homeland. Over the years, I had learned to embrace foods that once seemed unfamiliar or unappealing. As I stirred the bubbling curry, the rich aroma filled the room, a heady blend of coconut milk, spices, and pumpkin sweetness. I smiled to myself, realizing that what had once been a childhood aversion had transformed into one of my favorite meals. And this time, I was making it for David, my sweet husband, who had grown fond of the vibrant flavors of Thailand.

David entered the kitchen, the tantalizing scents drawing him in. His eyes lit up at the sight of me cooking. "Is that the pumpkin curry?" he asked, his voice filled with excitement as he inhaled the fragrant steam rising from the pot.

I chuckled, a hint of nostalgia in my voice. "Yes, it is. But I used to hate this when I was a kid," I admitted, stirring the curry as the colors swirled together beautifully. "The pumpkin always seemed too sweet, and the curry too spicy. I never liked it."

I paused, looking at him with a fond smile, the memories flooding back. "I think it's because I'm not a little girl anymore. I've learned to appreciate the flavors and love making it for you. It's like... a piece of home, something I can share with you," I said, my heart swelling with warmth.

David's expression softened at my words. He knew how much I had struggled with homesickness since moving to America. Still, moments like this—sharing my culture and traditions—brought us closer. "I love it," he said sincerely, his voice full of admiration. "I'm so lucky to have you and your cooking."

My eyes sparkled at his compliment. I added the final touches to the curry, a sprinkle of fresh basil releasing yet another layer of fragrant aroma. As I ladled the vibrant dish into bowls, David busily set the table, eager to share in the experience of this dish that had once caused childhood discomfort but had now transformed into a symbol of love and growth.

Sitting together, savoring the *Pumpkin Red Curry*, I realized how much I had changed. I had gone from dreading the dish to loving it, not just for its taste but for the memories and connections it carried. Each spoonful reminded me of my journey of embracing what once felt foreign. With David by my side, I had discovered a newfound appreciation for the things that had once seemed difficult, making me feel more at home than ever.

At that moment, I understood that food was more than just nourishment; it was a bridge connecting my past to my present, a celebration of love, growth, and the beautiful journey we were on together.

Pumpkin Red Curry

SPICES and SAUCES:

2 tablespoons Thai red curry

1 bunch Thai basil

2.5 tablespoons brown, or palm sugar

1 teaspoon salt

2 tablespoons fish sauce

INGREDIENTS:

1 pound pork shoulder, sliced into small thin bits

1 pound pumpkin or squash cubed

1 can coconut milk

7-8 kaffir lime leaves

DIRECTIONS:

- Add ¼ can of coconut milk to small pot over medium heat. Simmer for 5 minutes.
- Add red curry and mix for 3 minutes.
- Add pumpkin or squash to pot along with 1 cup of water.
- Add kaffir lime leaves, sugar, salt, and fish sauce.
- When pumpkin or squash is half-way cooked (approx. 8 minutes) add pork and remaining coconut milk. Mix well.
- When thoroughly cooked, turn off heat.
- Add Thai basil and mix.
- Serve in a bowl with cooked jasmine rice on the side.

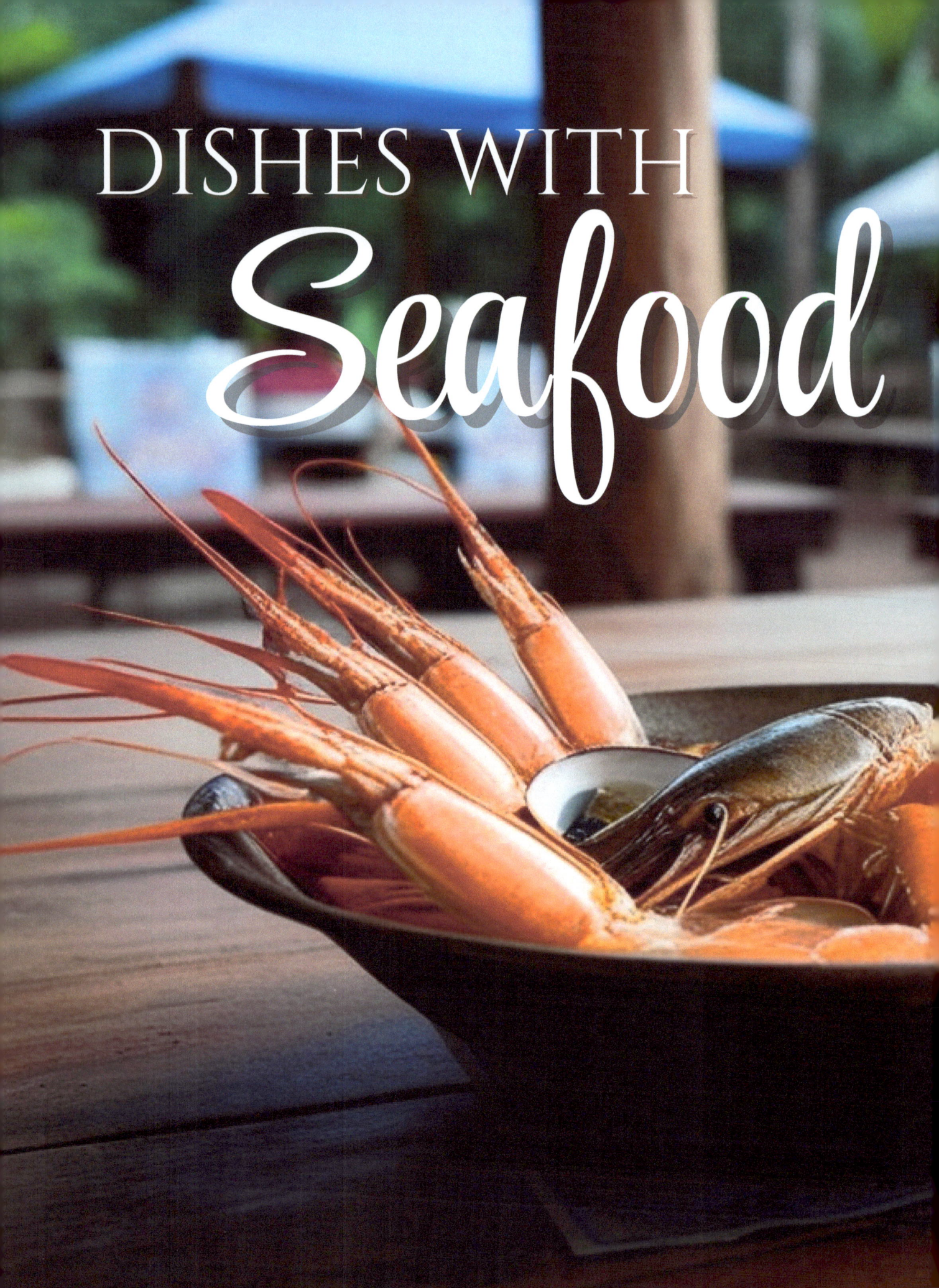

DISHES WITH
Seafood

Tom Yum Goong

Our love story began in a whirlwind of cultural differences, language barriers, and shared dreams of building a life together. From the moment our eyes first met, a spark ignited between us—an undeniable connection that defied the boundaries of our backgrounds. But it wasn't until we shared our first bowl of *Tom Yum Goong* together that we truly bonded, and that moment remains etched in my heart.

I remember that evening vividly. The kitchen was filled with the fragrant aromas of herbs and spices, a reminder of my Thai roots. My radiant smile must have mirrored the warmth in my heart as I introduced David to this beloved dish. *Tom Yum Goong*, a quintessential Thai dish, was more than just food; it was a piece of home, a tradition wrapped in memories of family gatherings and laughter echoing through the house.

At first, David hesitated, unsure of what to expect. He was not accustomed to such bold, complex flavors, and I could see the uncertainty in his eyes. But when he finally took that first spoonful, everything changed. The warmth of the broth enveloped him, and the kick of the chili, balanced by the bright notes of citrusy lemongrass, awakened his senses in a way he had never experienced before.

"Spicy!" he exclaimed, wiping his brow as the heat hit him. I couldn't help but laugh, watching him navigate the burst of flavors with pure delight. At that moment, I felt a rush of love and pride. He tried hard to embrace my culture, even if it meant getting a little red in the face. It was a beautiful sight, watching him savor the taste, and I realized that food had become our bridge—a way to connect our worlds.

As time went on, *Tom Yum Goong* became our special thing. It was our comfort food, a symbol of our growing love. Whether we faced challenges or celebrated milestones, we would sit down together, bowls steaming between us, and enjoy the vibrant, spicy concoction. Each spoonful reminded us how far we had come together—a journey that started with a little hesitation but blossomed into something profound and cherished.

Navigating life from different corners of the world was not always easy, but we found solace in our shared moments over that steaming bowl of soup. Through the laughter, the occasional tears, and the spice that sometimes made us gasp, we discovered a language all our own—a language of love that transcended words, expressed through our shared experiences and the comfort we found in each other's company.

No matter the obstacles, David and I knew our love was as strong and flavorful as the soup we shared on that unforgettable evening. Each bowl was a testament to our journey, filled with warmth, connection, and the promise of many more adventures. And in those moments, surrounded by the comforting aroma of *Tom Yum*, I knew we had created something beautiful together—an everlasting bond that would carry us through life, one spicy spoonful at a time.

Tom Yum Goong

SPICES and SAUCES:

10-15 cilantro

3-5 dried chilis

3-5 fresh Thai chilis - sliced

3 tablespoons fish sauce

1 tablespoon Thai chili paste

1 tablespoon brown sugar

INGREDIENTS:

1 pound raw shrimp

2-3 different types of mushrooms

10-15 pieces lemongrass - sliced

5-10 pieces sliced galangal

5 Kaflir lime leaves - stems removed

3-5 whole shallots

1 can condensed milk OR 1/2 can coconut milk

2 cups water

3 tablespoons fresh lime juice

DIRECTIONS:

- Heat water in pot over high heat.
- Add lemongrass, shallots and galangal, stir for 1 minute.
- Add mushrooms and shrimp, cook for 3-5 minutes, stirring frequently.
- Reduce heat to medium.
- Add condensed or coconut milk, chili paste, fish sauce, fresh chilis, sugar, lime juice.
- Turn temperature off.
- Serve in bowls, topping with dried chilis, Kalifir lime leaf, cilantro, and lime quarters.

Stir Fried Yellow Curry Seafood

I stood in the kitchen, my heart brimming with excitement as I prepared a dish that had captured my soul during a trip to Phuket: *Thai Seafood Stir-Fried Yellow Curry*. The aroma of spices and coconut milk filled the air, wrapping around me like a warm snuggle. It was one of those unforgettable moments from my vacation—the rich, creamy curry paired with the freshest seafood from the Andaman Sea had left a lasting impression.

The bold flavors, the perfect balance of spice, and the vibrant colors had stuck in my memory, a taste of home and adventure that I had promised to share with David one day. Today, that promise was finally being fulfilled.

David, who had come to love the unique flavors of my cooking, snuck into the kitchen, his curiosity piqued by the intoxicating scents wafting through the air. "What are you making today, my love?" he asked, his voice filled with eager anticipation.

My eyes twinkled with mischief as I stirred the bubbling pot. "*Yellow Curry Seafood*. It's from Phuket. I fell in love with it when I was there."

David's eyebrows raised, a playful grin forming on his face. "Seafood? Sounds a little fishy," he teased, half-joking but genuinely curious.

I laughed warmly, my confidence shining through. "Don't worry, it'll be perfect." I was determined. While I had made yellow curry before, this was different. This dish brought back memories of the salty breeze, the vibrant markets, and the incredible seafood of Phuket. It was a connection to the place I had cherished, and now, I was sharing it with the person I loved most.

As I stirred the curry, adding the creamy coconut milk and fragrant curry powder, the familiar warmth of the dish started to take shape. The rich, golden hue deepened. I could almost hear the waves crashing against the shore as I carefully added shrimp, mussels, and squid—my favorite seafood ingredients. Each addition brought me closer to recreating the dish that had captured my heart. The kitchen was filled with the fragrant aroma of garlic, ginger, and spices, mingling with the sweet scent of coconut. I could hear David's stomach growling in anticipation.

Finally, the curry was ready. I proudly ladled the creamy, seafood-filled goodness into bowls, the colors vibrant and inviting. David took his first bite, paused, and stared at me wide-eyed.

I held my breath for a moment, my heart racing with hope.

David looked at me with a smile, his eyes sparkling with delight. "This... this is amazing," he said, his voice full of surprise and joy. "You've really captured the taste of Phuket. It's like I'm right there with you."

My heart swelled with happiness. I had shared a piece of my journey with David, and it had brought us even closer. At that moment, surrounded by the warmth of love and the tantalizing flavors of home, I knew that no matter where life took us, we would always find our way back to each other—through food, memories, and the deep bond we shared.

The kitchen echoed with laughter and the clinking of bowls, a celebration of love infused with the essence of adventure. Each bite was a reminder of how far we had come together, and I felt grateful to share this piece of my heart with him.

Stir Fried Yellow Curry Seafood

SPICES and SAUCES:

3 tablespoons yellow curry powder

1 teaspoon brown or palm sugar

3 tablespoons light soy sauce

2 tablespoons oyster sauce

3 tablespoons cooking oil

1 teaspoon black pepper

1 1/2 tablespoons Thai chili paste

INGREDIENTS:

1 pound white shrimp, peeled and divided

1/2 clove garlic, peeled and chopped

3 eggs

1 onion, sliced

Chinese celery 1/2 bunch, sliced into 1 inch pieces

1/2 bunch spring onion, cut into 1-inch pieces

3-4 red peppers, sliced into small pieces

1 can evaporated milk

DIRECTIONS:

- Prepare 1 pound of shrimp (any seafood can be used).
- Add 2 tablespoons of the yellow curry powder into a bowl with Thai chili paste.
- Add sugar, soy sauce, oyster sauce, and 150 ml of milk.
- Heat cooking oil in Wok or frying pan on medium heat.
- Add garlic to oil, stir 30-45 seconds.
- Add shrimp, cooking until shrimp is half cooked.
- Add onion, 1 tablespoon of curry powder, and pepper.
- In separate bowl whisk eggs and add to Wok or frying pan.
- Stir until everything is well done and has a creamy look, about 4 minutes.
- Add celery, spring onion, and red peppers to the pan.
- Mix and cook for 1-2 minutes.
- Remove from heat and serve alone or with jasmine rice.

From Our Kitchen to Yours ...

The Secret Taste of Love is a heartfelt cookbook that intertwines Annie's cherished childhood memories from Thailand with her favorite recipes. It also intermingles Annie's and my lives, crafting a journey that celebrates both food and love.

As we share this book with you, we reflect on our shared passion for Thai cuisine, which has been a cornerstone of our relationship. Through personal stories and culinary adventures, we illustrate how cooking and food have deepened our bond. We encourage you to explore the vibrant flavors of Thai cuisine in your own kitchens because of the importance of preserving cultural heritage through food.

In addition to the recipes and stories, we reflect on our journey together, from the early days filled with challenges to building a life centered around love and mutual respect. We want to invite you to try the recipes and embrace the stories and traditions behind them, fostering a deeper appreciation for the cultural significance of food in bringing people together.

The Secret Taste of Love is more than just a cookbook; it's a narrative of love, culture, and the unifying power of food. We hope to inspire you to cherish your own culinary traditions and the relationships nurtured around the dining table.

We want to thank each and every one of you who has been a part of our journey over the past eight years. From our struggles as we came to America to inviting us into your homes, you have become family. We are grateful for all your support and love throughout this adventure. Thank you for being part of our extended family, and we look forward to sharing our lives with you as we continue this beautiful journey together.

Much Love,

David & Annie

www.ingramcontent.com/pod-product-compliance
Lightning Source LLC
Chambersburg PA
CBHW041549120626
46551CB00002B/155